Warmly,
The Wild

poems by

Emily Iris Degn

Finishing Line Press
Georgetown, Kentucky

Warmly,
The Wild

For Nick, my bear, forever partner and best friend. Thank you for your unconditional belief in me, beautiful heart, and courage that has taken us over Icelandic glaciers and volcanoes. You will always have my heart, my sweet love. I'm excited to keep telling stories at your side.

For Mama, who brought me into this world and has spent every moment since teaching me that nature is our church.

For Dad, who took me camping before I could walk and will always be my storm-watching companion.

For Abby, my very first friend who has walked beside me endless times across our little island.

For Liberty, whose wheatfield hair and fern facts brought so much magic to my childhood.

For William, my hiking buddy who will always be "Pal" to me no matter how grown up we get.

For George, my other explorer whose ability to make me laugh even with low blood sugar at the top of a mountain is sorcery.

For Daisy, who completes us and continues to love us no matter where we are.

For Kenny, who saw too few sunrises and yet still brings so much light to all of our lives.

For Grampy, who is the reason I never miss a sunset.

For Grandpa, who taught me to love others and the planet selflessly.

For Papa, who brought me home to the Salish Sea.

For every teacher who ever encouraged me to write, especially Mrs. Robbins and Mary, without whom this book would not be possible.

For Earth, which inspired my very first poem and continues to shape me as a writer and artist.

Finally, for the little girl I used to be, who talked to trees, collected rocks and leaves, stayed up late reading every night, filled the pockets of her overalls with flowers, and was convinced she'd write a book when she grew up. You did it, "Sunshine."

Copyright © 2025 by Emily Iris Degn
ISBN 979-8-89990-220-8 First Edition
All rights reserved under International and Pan-American Copyright Conventions. No part of this book may be reproduced in any manner whatsoever without written permission from the publisher, except in the case of brief quotations embodied in critical articles and reviews.

Publisher: Leah Huete de Maines
Editor: Christen Kincaid
Cover Art: Emily Iris Degn
Interior Art: Emily Iris Degn
Author Photo: Nicholas Allen Morgan
Cover Design: Emily Iris Degn

Order online: www.finishinglinepress.com
also available on amazon.com

Author inquiries and mail orders:
Finishing Line Press
PO Box 1626
Georgetown, Kentucky 40324
USA

Contents

Yule 1

What Came Before
    Piece of the Earth 5
    The Hum 6

Winter
    Kelp and Clay 9
    Awaited 10
    There were Once Hickory Trees Along this River 11
    Speak to the Calm 13
    Oak and Fire 14
    Imbolc 16
    Speak to the Storm 17
    Sputter Warmth 18
    Holding on to Winter 20
    They Grew Too 21
    In the Quiet of the Snowfall 24

Spring
    Ostara 27
    I Came Home to Fidalgo Island 28
    Stretching Towards the Sun 30
    The Ground 31
    Forsythia Bushes and the Sound of River Water 32
    Appalachia, in Blue 34
    Seaglass 35
    Pavement Breathing 37
    The Glow 38
    Beltane 39
    Barefoot Below Jardine Juniper 41

Summer
    Red Hills Along the Coast 45
    Litha 47
    So I Spin Here 48
    Canada was Burning 50
    Pines and Pacific 51
    I Watched the Eclipse with My Sisters 53
    Float 54
    Fraying Bark 55

A Globe of Oceans...56
There's Nature in the City 57
The Fields on Whidbey Island 59
A Different Kind of Genesis 60
Imagine the Warm Rain in the Humidity of Virginia 61
Lughnasadh 62
Anacortes, in Blue 64

Autumn

Conversing 69
Mabon 71
The Wild Grass We Cut Down 72
Shapes of Roots and Lightning 73
One Night When the Bears Came 75
Falling Gold 76
Lilac 77
Listening to the Hum 79
Inland in November 80
You will wonder 82

What Comes After

Eutrophication 85
Dear Out There, ...86

Yule

Morning soaks into the hills like a luscious marmalade.

As the tangerine light shimmers through the webbed branches,
the birch trees brush the mountains,
and I sit on vibrant skies to watch the sun come up.

I can see my breath.

In solace, I inhale and wait
for the blanketed grasses below the snow.
It will be a season before they stud the dirt with jade.

For now, I am e x h a l i n g —waiting
for them to grow
and come back to me.

I wonder how they learned that they can always come home eventually.

Like the trees, wild grasses don't die
when it's winter.
They sleep.

Just like you and me and all of us do when we're too tired

to hold our heads up.
We made our minds up
not to sleep,

when every living being has the word "Rest" written on their filaments.

Our planet always orbits fully,
and yet we think we know better than this—

enough to skip one of our own seasons.

What Came Before

Piece of the Earth

My palms are etched by Nature,
and cooled by the breath of trees
and atmosphere. I belong here—
Here in this cerulean orb, dipped in light.

I am the wild and the fight to see the sunrise.
I am this untamed glint of equatorial jungles and ice conversing.

I am bark and dawn and streams
warmly wrapped around this breathing thing,
this soul-filled being.
These purple veins are just roots, pumping blood and water.

I close my eyes to set the Sun in the evening hours, and bask
in shuttered shades of Fire.

I'm woven with the seams of land and sea and every one
of the forsaken prairies. This place tilts with my head bowing
in the twirling air. I carry dying pieces of Earth everywhere—
my arms and wrists and hands, stained with poisoned soil and extinct
    footprints.

The same mines that pit the Hillsides are dug into my body,

bare.

The Hum

The Earth is an aurora borealien hum,
set to the frequency of loss—
      a wine glass filled
      with blood, oceans, dirt, and trees;
          your cupped hands, dripping
          with salt water and rain and mud.

      She is the millisecond of your birth
        and that first breath that you sucked into your body, your
body the shape of a rosebud—raw and wrecked
from first light.

The Earth is a gulp of winking atmosphere and your pink, aging
skin—
the way the ice drifts further away from
its polar kin, until they can no longer whisper together.

      She is Endings and everything in between the two of us,
      and the etching of our sunward palms,
          tilted in praise for the warmth on our freckled shoulders.

      The Earth is the crystalized moon, filled with
      cratered hearts—pulverized from the gnashing teeth of
      wasted time, and blinking minds and funeral songs.

      She is our sand-crusted feet and the wash
      of a melted frost as the eager sproutlings stretch
through the soil.

The Earth is not dying

          but we are.

Winter

Kelp and Clay

Pines settle in
for the Long Gray, as they root themselves
on the shoreline. The madness of the seagull's song
wafts onto the sails and decks
of ocean-whipped men.
The fire of the Last Light
douses their smile-creased cheeks with copper.
There is a certain enchantment
in the way evening gold spills from a lighthouse,
and onto the carpeted fog on the coast.
There is certain order in the chaos-riddled pattern
of kelp and clay, at their feet.

Awaited

Caked in snow, the lane
breathes while the sky whispers
in quiet flurries, sagging with armfuls
of a weighted gray, and the promise of an
awaited daylight season.

Hushed branches ice themselves, sparkling
like tufts of cotton. The roadside forest learned to glisten
during the darkness of periwinkle and charcoal shades.

Withered brown leaves and pine needles braid the surface
of this snow-laden lane—the pavement cracking below
as it braves the dipping temperatures.

On this gentle night, it will snow again,
covering the fallen things, the withered leaves,
and the things we paved over.

There Were Once Hickory Trees Along This River

We decided a long time ago that Hickory Trees were good for lumber.

Their hearty bark that holds their skin together
is something we hack apart and spatter in slivers across the snow.
Long ago we decided that they would flavor the flesh of those we kill,
and that they would be the handles of the tools we used to do it.

A mighty Tree now known as "wood chips"—the Rivers cry and flood
their deforested banks over this.

Did we bother to get to know them—to ask them
how it feels to sway with every windstorm until the stillness comes back
again? Do we wait like them for our leaves to grow back, or do we retract
every vulnerable thing we say? Did we even bother to kneel down before
them and ask if it's okay

to let them down? We never counted the rings they grew as they got older or
learned what any of it even means. Did we learn that we could gather Hickory
nuts when the months got colder? No. Just the same, we turned them into
   things.

We knew they could be used as lumber before we knew their names.

I Fall Asleep to Creek Water Songs

Speak to the Calm

This is the first year that the creek outside our home froze over.
The running water stilled, and snow collapsed onto the pavement beside it
in a lather of cloud-made suds and clumps of ice.

The dark violet sky hushes this place,
as a silence swallows the rooftops beneath the blinking galaxies.

Does it snow somewhere in the unlit corners of space?
Or is that just here—just us here, in this vacuum interlaced
with orbital traces and rips in the fabric?

There are colossal dances and collisions above this—
above the tree branches that hold the weather coming down,
and the wounds we give them. We sleep outside
to feel closer to It All.
That's a lot to put on the shoulders of trees.

Planets spin and bow and collapse in on themselves up there,
as this balcony fills up with twinkling snowflakes.
The sky exhales in stillness.

Our window panes are painted with mist, because the Winter
likes to paint with her breath.

There are trails of deer prints in the field out there,
leading to the forest that I speak to every day,
complaining that there isn't enough nature for me to say things to.

Oak and Fire

My foggy morning eyes search the indigo
pine lines
as they meet the looking-glass tide.
Coffee stains my teeth with oak and fire,
while I sing the song of an early sunrise.

January on the Sound

Imbolc

Morning river air prickles on the surface of my cheeks.
Trickling creeks harmonize with whispers of the leaves
rustling against the sky.
My eyes stream up deep canyons
etched into the bark of the chestnut oak,
and land on the branches that brush the glistening dawn.

Life spurts from the stray roots,
and curls around my feet.
Water flows like wild hair,
and the crisp breath of the early hours
coats my fingers in a welcomed ice.

Leaves coat the soggy soil below,
resembling the back of a leaf-feathered raven.
Newborn grass sprouts forth from the banks—
these shreds of spring nudging our snowed-in souls.

Speak to the Storm

Clouds and sea mist painted with stone,
and the drop of rain that stalls the still.
Let out your tales, with the wail
of water-logged winds.

Speak to the storm.

Sputter Warmth

Champagne snow simmers with each hungry foot
fall, and I gulp
down mouthfuls of dense air.

February coated my thoughts so far this year—
like frosting spread onto a warm olive oil cake.

The little breath of a breeze entangles
itself in my hair, and sleeves my sun-drawn arms.
The sky is drenched in a passionate blue, and trains of clouds

sp ut ter

across the expanse.
Elms are entangled in honey above my head,
and the sunlight drips onto my crown.
I'm bathed in something that I've gone months without-

warmth.

Mount Baker at Sunrise

Holding on to Winter

Winter trickles down the wall's vines,
lonely in the arriving blooms.
It clings to waning cold spells, and hopes

to pause the moon.

February dies in mourning,
as the lunar rush tugs March forward.
The trees haven't flowered yet,

and snow's Death is coming
soon. The cold, now burned, surrenders,
and gives in to Springtime's gloom.

They Grew Too

My socks are wet from melting snow—stained by oil puddles and pavement.
Carrying canvas bags of food, I think about the payment of It All.
My shoulders ache from the weight of the haul,
and I wonder where the food came from.

It grew.

It grew like millions and billions of plant things
do, and they do it for free.
A Blue Jay floats away from a mulch-grown tree,
catching the wind to swoop to the parking spaces.
His throne is a dented green car.

I don't understand how people think they are better than winged beings
like him. We know how to drive and cook and how nuclear fusion works,
but does that make up for what we do to each other and to the forests where
we used to live with birds? We used to know that existence is worth
celebrating on its own, and then we got bored and tired.

We complicated the mere act of staying alive.

The Blue Jay eats like I do, but none of the other birds make him
pay for it. I wonder what he'd say if they tried to.
He wouldn't stand for it.

The penniless and full-bellied bird watches as I reach
my car. I think he knows how lost we are—how far away we feel
from home. We grew these little trees after we paved over
what was here, and still don't know where to find bits of nature.

I get into the car as the other birds talk to each other,
no doubt saying "Look at this creature
who doesn't know what she's here for, or where to find food.
Watch her ignore the shade this tree gives her. She forgets it wasn't made—

it grew".

And I guess parking lot trees are not dead.
Their birds can sing too,
and they're a forest no matter what we call them,
or whether or not we put a superstore beside them.

They also bloom.

Ancestral Rocks

In the Quiet of the Snowfall

When Grandpa died, I went to the woods
outside my home. I was wearing pajamas
when I found out, so I pulled on boots
and a warm coat, and ran to the cover of trees.

I cried and held the leafless guardians,
burying myself in the icy fog and distant calls of geese.

I kept coming back, finding that in this palace of branches,
I felt safe to mourn.

The sound of my boots cracking icy snow beneath them
became Grandpa's voice. The frothy snowflakes floating
to the ground became the morning light drifting into
his kitchen, stocked with my favorite breakfast cereals. Holding
the forest, tree by tree, became the way I got to still hug him.

He became these woods, despite him having died across the country
in Oregon. I'd get up before the sunrise, and just sit
where the Eastern Hemlock and Redcedar were densest. It felt
like sitting on his living room floor. I could almost hear him
telling me to not take adults too seriously. He used to leap into the Pacific so
    freely.

I knew he wasn't in these woods.
I knew he couldn't be.

But as the snow fell quietly that winter, I'd forget his ashes were spread in a
river and forest, so far away from me. He always wanted to be returned to the
Earth in the end.

I still go to the woods when I miss him, and I smell that oceanic scent
of his house and the lemon tree outside.
But maybe he is gone; no bit of him left to speak to or hold.
Or maybe this Earth is just bark and ash and the souls of those who loved us.

Spring

Ostara

Almond blossoms ice the tree
in frothy, pink foam.

It looks like the branches dipped themselves into strawberry milk.

They're thin enough to break,
and fly
away in the coming winds

like rose-colored swans.

I Came Home to Fidalgo Island

A Red-Winged Blackbird perches
in the reeds and wetlands,
as a morning fog weaves its way among the Shore Pines.

The faint smell of last night's
campfire distills itself into the black dirt,
and into my hair, spun
and woven with dew and clementine shades.

I walk towards the water line.
Oysters are rolled by the tide onto the soggy beach,
and I gulp down breaths of the cold Pacific air.

I remember as a kid going everywhere with sandy
oyster shells in my pockets. My pants were always covered in the sea,
but I loved it—marine salt and bits of kelp caked on my feet
like a pair of impractical shoes.

I'd wash them off in the marsh on the way home,
only to walk through the oozing mud from rain the night before—
our hardwood floors suffered, I'm sure.

I wonder what would happen if I still kept oyster shells in my pocket.

I pick one up, and it shines and ripples like the water that houses it.
The cold calcium carbonate feels like a totem in my hand.
I burrow my feet a little deeper into the wet sand.

It feels like I'm holding a piece of who I used to be—
that free little girl who lived by the sea;
who tossed her head back to yell and scream and plea
that the orcas would be safe and grow old alongside her.

I'm older now and their numbers have grown smaller,
and my shrinking pockets can't hold oyster shells anymore.
But the Red-Winged Blackbird still perches in the reeds and wetlands.

Blue Season in the San Juan Islands

Stretching Towards the Sun

Looking up, I see thin branches clasping their hands together like a braided pastry.

The blue hills swoop down to the forests,
and occasionally-dotted homes that border the campus.

The sky sleeps above in shades of an approaching evening rain.

I breathe it in, under the magnolia trees.
Their crystallizing buds glint like holiday lights,
each one the color of the silvery river.

Tufts of grass lay on top of eager roots—like mossy sheets of emerald pooling beneath my feet. The birds around me sound like chimes as they sing to the Earth.

The dirt isn't frozen anymore.

The Ground

An olive-tinted bush bristles against
the rush of after-hours.

4:30 p.m. is the growing time.

Its roots are clotted with chunky soil,
and its leaves look like wax paper.
The oily shades of evergreen
lap the underbellies of the greenery,

and plastic cutlery
and gum wrappers decorate The Ground.

Forsythia Bushes and the Sound of River Water

I met him in the crafting aisle of Walgreens.
The trees outside were blooming, and I found myself walking
miles every day just to spend more time with them. Flowering
Cherry. Dogwood. Redbud. Magnolia.
Right before sunset, their vibrant pink and white would turn the color of
 forsythia.

We fell in love talking about the pleasure of eating
apple butter, and the way the rain smells on the east coast.
It was in the rain that we kissed each other for the first time,
and it kept raining. When I told him I loved him,
there was a rainbow glowing through the 5 p.m. storm outside
our windows. His sparkling eyes looked like the Earth in spring—
warm shades of espresso and willow tree bark. When it got dark,
we made up stories about the stars.

We sat on the flooding river, on a fallen log
with roots tethered to the shore. We feasted on
strawberry jam and peanut butter sandwiches, and watched
the water eat away the muddy riverbanks.
Now the sound of river water sounds like home to me.

Poseidon Plays in the Foam

Appalachia, in Blue

If you dug beneath the dirt, here in the mountains,
you'd find money in the form of oil.

You'd find rusty, leaking pipes,
and greed's cigarette butts.

If you walked around,
you'd see the absence of the torn-down farmhouses
from the turn of the century. Some are older—were older.
It didn't matter. They needed the land they were on anyway.

They shave the heads of the mountaintops here.

The blue, ancient, peaks are ragged and wild when they're left to
    breathe.
The rivers braid themselves between the Eastern White Pines.
There are plenty of berries to forage on here.

All the while the Blue Catfish and Warmouth are dying,

but it's still beautiful. We live in the middle of It All—
folded between the hills, and bear dens and thousands of waterfalls.
The land around us is scarred, and it's not hard to see that it's still
    bleeding.

Seaglass

I find solace
in the far colors of the sky,
and between the folds of my outdoor words,
and the moment before the sun rises.

I am a mess of intentions.

I hide my feelings in rain puddles,
and in walks along streams,
and in the way I dream of oyster shells
and green bottles that have shattered into sea glass.

In the Green Light of Virginia

Pavement Breathing

I learned recently that New York City rises 14 inches every day,
twice a day. Land tides; Earth tides.
The moon's gravity provides the pull,
and when it's directly above Central Park,
it's high tide. 14 inches. Sink and rise.
It's breathing pavement.
Inhale. Exhale. Reprise.
As the moon moves across the planet, everything below it grows
to reach it. Gravity lessens, and a spine of risen land
rolls across the Earth in a terrestrial wave.
The subway stations and art galleries and fire escape gardens
all stand a little taller. And no one feels a thing.

The Glow

Sunlight warms my forehead.
It feels like the taste of orange juice
after a breathless run by the river.

The solar heat wraps me in gold,
and I melt into The Glow of everything.

Beltane

I came looking for Honeysuckle, thinking of my evening tea.
Points of light filter through the leaves that flit below the glowing sky.
I carry the basket that I got when I was eight or nine—the one I used to
fill with twigs and leaves that I admired.

I think that a smaller version of me would like this riverbed
filled with squawks and the cackle
of bird conversations. I know I'd try to join in,
without a question. I only do that now when no one's here.

I forage and watch as silky-headed ducks putter through the currents
along the shore. Canadian Geese victoriously parachute onto the water,
with wings outstretched and feet skidding along the surface.
On the riverbed you can hear it—the drum of the turtles' heartbeats.

Willows wave in a soft breeze, and a butterfly floats
like cotton on the prairies. My basket is full but I stay
for the wild berries, listening to the rustle
of the Golden Hour gulping down the day.

Smithfield Canyon

Barefoot Below Jardine Juniper

Periwinkle mounds tumble across the horizon—
an ocean of dusty peaks and ridgelines.
Scents of Sagebrush and Junipers
seep into my sky-faded flannel.

My palms are caked
in callouses and Earth,
coated in life and pieces
of tree-lined beginnings. I watch as the stretching
arms of Yellow Fixweed reach for each other.

Can you hear the elevation's air pulsing through the canyon?

I climb up higher each time to see if swaying meadow grass
looks smaller from here. It feels larger than life when I run down there—
there below the Aspen trees and snow-splashed mountains.
I like to leap down the wild foothills like I'm a deer trying to catch the wind.

Did you know that you can find seashells in these mountains?

All of them remind me that once, the sea forsook the shore.
I once tore my pockets because I tried stuffing them with more
land-crusted shells than they could hold. Now I try to leave them untouched.
Do the falling bark and foaming pine needles speak to the whispering
underbrush, or is that just the sound of my bare footsteps—tearing the Earth
with my presence?

Summer

Red Hills Along the Coast

Rose petal sunsets glisten on the surface
of the sea, as the Californian scarlet blooms
sway with the warm breeze.

It's wildfire season.

Watching the Sun Slip in San Diego

Litha

I dance under the glitter of our midsummer
bonfire. Every spark spitting dissolves into solar light.
As I kick the dirt with my bare and dust-kissed feet,
I imagine my ancestors of the north dancing
with me. Chanting. This is the day that the
sun stands still. Solstice.

So I Spin Here

She lives in the space between your thoughts
and her realities. She drinks in the atmosphere
like it's the sea gulping down glacial melt.

    She chokes on your rephrased truths and poison.

        She weaves worlds with her heartstrings
        as you carve your grocery lists, gas bills and hymns
        into her giving palms. She holds forests on her shoulders.

    What have you done, with that fire that smells like the stars?

She dances with Jupiter
while you chew on the death you bring to others.
As she offers to wash your feet

        in warm woodland mud and ocean salt, you offer her piles
        of old habits and stolen rocks eternally. She sings you Psalms
        of Solemn Men—crushed under the land you took from them.

    She sings you lost ballads of hornless beasts you think you're better than.

    You tuck yourself into bed with stolen years.
    You can silence holy whispers. You shut your doors to her
questions and your Old Fears and Testaments.

What will you do when your Last Suppers rot the air?

    Who will catch the mountains when they fall
    in sheets of sliding water? Which land will you move to
    when yours is stolen by your choices?

        The drowned islands of the east,
        or the brittle deserts of the west?
        The starved tundras of the north,
        or the muddy footprints that used to be snow?

Where will you go?

Her arms out-stretch
with marigold Eves between them,
and she holds the wet clay of shorelines that still exist.

    I hope your mouth is full when your home-grown rivers die.

        I hope your belly is fed when the last exotic animal is
        dead. I hope you remember them and lie in shreds
        of the wild that you kept for yourself

    in caged zoos and tideless pools and ancient oil cans.

I hope you think it was worth it
when you cough up your soul and feed it to your habits.
I hope the jungle keeps you warm that you set on fire in return for snacks,

    but you should know you're a pyromaniac in the worst of ways.

        Flattering yourself, by painting your actions
        green, won't resurrect the death you've dealt out to your
        descendants when you dug them an early grave with a
        cleaver.

    So I spin here

un-Earthed and re-named,
and I'm sorry to say you'll join me if you remain the same,
and I wish you all the best.

Canada Was Burning

I sit on the beach of my little island,
and watch the skies across the bay turn pink.
They carry armfuls of humidity—something we don't
usually have this far up north.

The sun is dipped in blood,
and sets fire to the grass.

Its red reflection ripples on the tides
of glassy ocean water below,
as it sinks behind the hazy island mounds.

For the first time, this far up north, the air is smoke.

Pines and Pacific

Cold morning air whispers
around my arms and legs,
like dew-struck spiderwebs.

The golden sunlight warms
the pine needles, and the amber-colored bark.

These woods are dense with
bird songs and morning dreams.

Wading through evergreens,
I kindle in the honey-light
on my skin.

The twinkling woods fade
into coasts, and blue-eyed oceans.

The glimmering waves greet my Earthen feet,
and I breathe in the air—

saturated with wildness.

Cascadian Gold

I Watched the Eclipse with My Sisters

The silver lunar smile
is swallowed by the Universe,
and a glassed-in continent.

The Moon's umbra spills Outer Space onto the Earth's surface,
like a dark wine. We look up at our dimming sky.

We are small dustings
inside the green path that we call
Totality.

Float

Pacific tides guide my kelp-tangled eyes to shore.
The violet tidal pools and barnacle—
studded rocks bear our name—the one the Earth sings to us.

Her name.

The roll and drag of tumbling waves
wrap around my ankles and sandy wrists. Periwinkle skies
dissolve into oceans and seas.

We are all made of each other.

We are the coast and sea otters and every one of the seven quintillion grains
of sand. We are the lavender dawn that coats the riptides and the hands
of those who love us most.

Ebony nights on the shore float
like seafoam; float like the salt that we keep
inside us.

Fraying Bark

I wake to moondust
on my eyelashes, and pine needles in my hair.
Wet leaves cling to my toes,
and all the while the forest breathes.

The sun is starting to rise,
on the oak trees and their fraying bark.

The dirt smells like cloves
and citrus, and I can hear eagles
cry above the branches.
Wild blueberries stud the ground.

As I pick my breakfast,
I don't mind staining my fingers with the vibrant juice.
It looks like my eyes.

A Globe of Oceans

The hills that I climb are waves
like the sea that I walk towards.

The blue splash below simmers into the air
around me, creating a globe of oceans.

The sunshine feels like freshly picked raspberries,
pesto sandwiches, and overalls torn
from kneeling in the dirt.

The sky is the same color as my old bedroom.

Cotton wisps of clouds
and blue herons twirl around the horizon
together.

The motion of each hill reminds me why I live along the shore.

There's Nature in the City

Soaked floral vendors top the sidewalk with roses.
Puddles of acrylic rainwater pool on the pavement
like ponds, and the marble storefronts glisten contentedly.

Paint spills over the city
and millions of clinging lights melt
into the rooftop gardens and cafe tablecloths.

A quiet rush hour saturates the world in rain,
and drenches the city in the dusky atmosphere.

Blue Magic in Tony Grove

The Fields on Whidbey Island

Lavender steam sinks into my skin.
Sunkissed and starry-eyed, I walk
barefoot through the blooming fields.

My feet are caked in Earth.

I gulp down breaths of Floral and vanilla notes,
And tuck fragrant sprigs behind my ear.
The land is magenta.

A Different Kind of Genesis

A stripe of desert holds up the setting sun,
and rust-colored boulders cup pools of the pink light.
My feet tumble across their oxidized, rocky palms, and my father passes me
in a blur of copper. We have the same hair color now that his scarlet has faded.
My own curls flop against my back as I fly towards the canyon's mouth.
My hair used to be long enough to brush against my hips, but it was too heavy.

I've never been good at letting go.

I used to pick up every rock I saw as a child.
I kept them in boxes and drawers around my bedroom.
When it came time to move, I filled a cardboard box with them,
and labeled it definitively as "rocks". I couldn't lift it, so when my mother
realized that it was the heaviest box packed, she told me to pick five
and leave the rest.

I've never been good at letting go.

So as I grew up, my hair kept growing too,
and then there came a point when I realized it was a part of me.
It terrified me to be so attached; to wonder if a small bit of me would die if I
    cut my hair.
So in an act of a different kind of genesis, I ended it—
the growing.

I cut it all off.

People protested, but I watched, mesmerized, as my hair fell.
What was left coiled up into the curls of my childhood,
like Fiddleheads.
I felt like I could float up to Orion,
with all the weight gone.

So now, a week before I leave home, my father and I are racing.
My mother stands nearby with her beautiful dark hair,
warmed by the sunset. She takes our photo as we sprint past her.
Red rock. Red hair.
We run through the desert, trying to see who is the first one to touch the sun.

Imagine the Warm Rain in the Humidity of Virginia

Tumbling thunder rolls through my valley
home. The Black Walnut trees quiver
and the mountains shake.
Robins race to the trees
as the storm snakes towards Salem.

Lughnasadh

In solar ceremony, I braid wild rye,
too distracted to think about anything
but the fact that today I saw an ad for a cruise line
that excitedly promised to provide:
"Incredible views of icebergs, crumbling into the ocean".

Watering the Salmon

Anacortes, in Blue

Indigo mountains crest
like waves
over my sea-kissed town.
Orca songs and kelp streamers greet the tangerine dawn.
Eagles cry and stud the sky in feathers
and airborne dreams.

Can you hear the scream of the salmon, dammed from the sea?

Deer meet with walking people like they're heading to a garden
party, and bushes carry armloads of moon-sized blackberries,
and thorns. An old wooden ship sits
marooned on the anemone-coated rocks
below the Ferry Road.
She carries pines on her shoulders
now, and an overload of myths
deemed true by passing tourists.

Seaglass glitters on our shores in foamy
hues, and rain and mist water the island
In Blue. Porpoises swim beside rainbow-colored kayaks,
and lilacs
and lavender keeps rhododendron bushes company.

Each summer gets hotter,
despite our ancient way of sweater-wearing junes.
We name the seals that glide through the Sound and blues.

We name the sailboats.
We name the storms that take them.

We name each other and the islands we live on,
and we think we can keep them
safe, but they get warm,

and littered on,

and suffocated by distant dams and violent laws,

and our trees,
and our gardens,
and our salmon and our whales,
and our seabirds,
and our tulip fields, and our wild keep dying,

and the world moves on—away from our little island.

Autumn

Conversing

Red clay bakes itself
onto my earthing feet. The ground
speaks to me
and reminds me that I am dirt
and stardust. I am nothing
and everything converse-
sing.

Aspens Dot My Childhood

Mabon

I sit in autumn's glory,
with foliage cascading down my neck and back.
Blue eyes, now studded with gold leaf.

Black ebony coating the flight of each raven.

Auburn squirrels chatter like waterfalls,
as I feast on September.

The Wild Grass We Cut Down

Mud-licked feet
fall on the spongy forest floor.
The smell of orange peels and fir drifts
through the pine needles
and swirls around my fingertips.

Earth and fire—an autumn
child.

The tilt of the land
grounds me,
as I walk into my soul.

The clouds embrace and frost the tops
of the trees.
I kneel and look up
at the ceiling of the universe.

I am made of mountaintops and glaciers spilling freely
from their cradle.

I am bark and roots
of trees. I am the wild grass we cut down
and the deer we slaughter.
Nature exists for the sake of being and nothing more,

and that tells me more about living than those living ever will.

Shapes of Roots and Lightning

I was born in October.

I speak the same tongue as shrinking leaves who crackle
and carpet the bruised sidewalk.

I never liked that I was born in the dying season,
because I wasn't taught to honor my darkness.

A life isn't just a birth. It's a death too—so in death there is aliveness.

Constructural Law explains why you and I have the shape of branches on our
bodies. Our lungs and palms and wrinkles all mirror lightning
and cracks of a droughted land. To be alive is to hold energy in our hands.

Look at the weaving of rivers and the run-off of melted snow.
Look at the roots below the starved dirt.
We are carbon from stars and energy from the Earth, and we get to keep it all
until we finish circulating that flow, and die.

In autumn time the trees don't stop existing,
but instead release the dying bits of themselves,
so they can greet the snow and then the spring.

I dance in the darkness, learning to nod to the death I hold as energy passes
    through me.

To have foliage and let it drop is a meditation in wholeness
that we've yet to master—the art of letting yourself die to come back home.

The Storm Came in From the Gulf

One Night When the Bears Came

There's a black bear who walks her children
to the creek outside my home.
Every full moon she does this,
as the forest parts for her.

I watch as I infuse my moon water
with my thoughts. She drinks,
and I ask myself why I never have the energy
to clean up this balcony anymore—rotting plants from
summertime still sitting in their pots.

Her children bumble forward into the light,
joining their mother at the banks.
I remember that I forgot to water my houseplants today,
again. We make ourselves be as productive in the darkening months,
as we are in seasons of full sunlight, and then wonder why we fail.

The bears drink from the creek together,
and I'm envious. It's inconvenient being
a person in a world where people
decided that water needed to have a price on it.
It's just outside my home and I can't drink it there.

But tonight the air smells like nutmeg,
and I can't tell if it's coming from my house
or the woods—dressed in ruby and copper.
The bears lumber back to the trees after an hour.

I wish they stayed.

Falling Gold

Dawn evaporates in curls of steam
from my morning
cup of tea, as the auburn leaves
rustle outside, perched
on branches like autumn-
shaded ravens and the wind
dances with the sky.

Let's run along the beach
side and inhale sea-salted
air like the gulls up there,
with their crackling throats
and outstretched wings to the pine
lines and little cries
from the dirt
and Earth we've stuffed
with our insecurities.

"Listen to me," scream the violet
sea stars seeing this violence of ours
as the atrocity it is, and hoping
that their tidal pool home
will be left alone and safe
from our claims and forced chains,
and all the while the sun
comes up and soaks the fog
in Gold.

Lilac

Leaves lay like crumpled grocery lists
on the lawn. Few still grasp onto the branches
and edges of their spindly tree.

I breathe hazelnut

as I step into the late autumn air.
The sky is bare and
lilac.

Logan Canyon

Listening to the Hum

Did you know that deep in the mountains you can hear the pull of the moon?

Its gravity is the only sound you can hear in those ancient places. Have you ever heard complete silence before?

I haven't. I'm not even sure what that would sound like—the absence of It All. Is it lonely to only have the gravitational pull of the moon to keep you company,
or is the sound reminding you

that even in the depths of rock and granite, your breath is not the only sound there?

How can anyone know that and not fall in love with this planet?—our planet, filled with the sounds of a hum we are just now discovering.

Inland in November

Looking through the tear-streaked window,
the rainfall seeps through the swollen skies.
The beautiful sadness of it strikes me as familiar,
as the pines sag with the heavy mist.

The birds abandon their lovers and leave,
and the jewel-toned leaves lay drowned on the ground.
The trees now stand barren and

alone.

All the while the sky pours out her soul and drenches us in her emotion.

The Leaves Shimmered

You will wonder

why your knees aren't smudged with grass anymore; why
you no longer long for the pour of a cold rain. Why
don't you jump into puddles anymore, letting the sky wash your feet?
You do jump still, but over them—as if you need to keep yourself
warm, when your hair and jacket are already soaked through.

You will wonder what got into you
when you threw out your dreams of playing
hopscotch on the moon. "There's no air up there" you argued, but

when's the last time you felt breathless?

Let me tell you this—it's probably been too long. Do you get along
with the trees? Or do you tune out their pleas
to let them help you? You want to breathe? Stop
cutting them down.

> Have you learned yet what their rings say, or are they just hardwood floors to you now?

You step on the heads of forests, and I'll tell you this now: You will wonder.
You will wonder when you're going to drown as the Atlantic
covers your favorite beach towns and hometowns in saltwater.
You hover over this irreversible phase. The "Tipping Point"
isn't far away—it's now. Eight years until the livable world falls down.
Your knees will be grass-smudged then, when you learn
about the last of us going up in flames. What do you gain
by setting your own house on fire?

You will wonder how you can plea to the wild to stay, when you're the one
who kicked yourself out. You'd rather leave than be small
without a doubt. You don't even hesitate. Please hesitate and look around,
because someday when I'm asked about the beings who covered the prairies
and foliage and glaciers in gasoline, I'll have to say: "I don't know, and I don't
think they knew who they were either".

> We used to have autumns and it's become clearer that it's too warm for that now.

What Comes After

Eutrophication

We live on a globe of Oceans.
We live by the swirling tides.
Our hours are gifted by a golden orb,
and to the Moon we let ourselves cry.
The Stars are bathed in atmosphere.
The Pacific sprays and the Atlantic sighs.

Our lungs are filled by the Sea and our hands cup her insides.

We hold the Planet in our arms. We hold ourselves at the same time.
As we choke the blues and greens down here,
we suffocate the Skies.
The Ocean bears our names and songs.
The Ocean bares our aging fates.

Less than a decade before it's too late for us.

There's a Dead Zone in the Gulf of Mexico.
We've taken the oxygen from our Sea and let the death grow.
There are people you know who believe that none of this is happening.
Find me a species who doesn't know that this is an emergency.
Find me another animal who sets their own habitat on fire.

If we keep burning down our home, it will stop existing.

Dear Out There,

I crave The Wild.

I crave the way the sun coats the desert
in jasper shades.
I crave the treelines.
The way the air grows cold and thin
makes me feel light
enough to fly.

I crave the sky.

A blanket of stars is free Out There.
Space is priceless.
I crave being known
as simply *Anonymous*;
to slip by
sea-sprayed coasts and sagebrush
without a word, because my insides
are exalting praise to the expanse.
Songs course through my heart and under my nature skin,

but I crave the silence.

The Wilderness never asks
questions or demands paychecks.
There is a resounding scream that exists
in that—"Out There!" "Out There!"

Out There,
I am unchained.
Out There, I wander—wordless,
because the crashing waterfalls take all there is to say.

I crave the new light of day;

light dancing on huckleberries and
my waking eyes;
the way the reaching mountains
cannot decide

whether or not they are blue
or violet gray.

I crave the fray

of Redwood bark
in the mist-laden rain.
The way I can sift through rivers
and croaks of swaying frogs,
without pause. Out There the air is ours—
not theirs to be sold for paper
or for gold.

I crave the rushing winds on my face

as I bury myself deeper
into The Wild—Out There.
I want to be tucked into the folds
of whispering forests
and age-old, creekbed stones.

I want to be alone and just

b r e a t h e in sync with All Of This
like we used to.
I want to wander through the blues and greens
that match my eyes and branching veins.
I miss it when we were free;
When we didn't have to carve our names on trees
because we remembered that
all of our names are the same as the Earth.

Warmly,
The Wild

Emily Iris Degn is a multilingual nature poet and artist, eco-travel writer, photographer, fiction writer, climate journalist, and essayist. Her writing has been nominated for the Best of the Net award, and her creative pieces can be found in many places, including *About Place Journal, Stonecrop Magazine, Capsule Stories, Lunch Ticket, Coffin Bell Journal, Coffee People Zine, Brick Street Poetry, Beyond Queer Words, On Concept's Edge, Salmon Creek Journal, Tipton Poetry Journal, For Women Who Roar,* and beyond. As a journalist, she has worked with *Explore Washington State, Tripoto, Luxury Daily, Taylor Magazine, Peaceful Dumpling, Borgen Magazine, Great Lakes Review, Arrivedo, Vegancuts, The New York Times* (in collaboration with *Luxury Daily*), *Bon Appétit* (in collaboration with *Luxury Daily*), among others.

With degrees in Environmental Studies, Creative Writing, and Art History, concentrating in Gender Studies at Roanoke College, Emily has spent her entire career working to forge a connection between readers and the planet through the humanities, believing that this will be the key to effective and widespread climate action. As an ecofeminist, she tells stories grounded in Earth and themes of wildness. She is deeply inspired by the work of scientists and those on the ground working to protect the Earth. Emily seeks to translate highly technical concepts into creative works, her nature poetry, land art, flash fiction, paintings, and photography. She pairs this very analytical part of the environmental emergency with the emotional aspect to capture a holistic picture of what it means to exist in transforming, fleeting landscapes.

Emily is from the Salish Sea in the Pacific Northwest but grew up exploring the continent with her parents, four siblings, and dog. As a child, she was fascinated by the planet, and could often be found star gazing, using her watercolor set to create jungle scenes, collecting rocks, climbing trees, reading through her Grandpa's giant stack of *National Geographic* magazines, and laying in the grass to be at eye level with bugs. She was also always a storyteller, frequently crafting poems and short stories. When she was 11 years old, she began routinely writing nature poetry, winning a state competition a few years later for her piece about a tree that she loved very much.

As an adult, Emily has explored widely, from living in the Atlantic Forest region of Brazil at 19 to backpacking through Iceland with her partner to road-tripping coast-to-coast across the continental United States many, many times. The time she spends in the Arctic continues to influence her work, being the land of her ancestors and one of the frontline regions of the climate crisis. It was on her North American journeys that she wrote *Warmly, The Wild*, but this international perspective is referenced throughout the collection.

When Emily isn't writing or making art, she can be found traveling, kayaking, playing in the woods, or reading about outer space, owls, and other things that blow her mind. She lives with her incredible partner Nick and their beloved book collection in Seattle. To follow along on her adventures, you can find her at @emilyirisdegn or @emfallstoearth on Instagram, or www.emilyirisdegn.com.

www.ingramcontent.com/pod-product-compliance
Lightning Source LLC
Chambersburg PA
CBHW042130160426
43198CB00022B/2971